The Battle of Talana

20 October 1899

Pam McFadden

RAVAN PRESS

The Battle Book Series

- The Battle of Talana
- The Battle of Elandslaagte
- The Battle of Colenso
- The Battle of Spioenkop
- The Battle of Vaalkrans
- The Battle of the Thukela Heights
- The Siege of Ladysmith

First published in 1999

Ravan Press
P O Box 145, Randburg 2125
© Pam McFadden

ISBN: 0 86975 480 7

DTP and design by: Heather Brooksbank, Resolution

Cover Design: David Selfe, Dark Horse Design

Cartography: Toni Bodington & Olive Anderson
    Cartographic Unit, University of Natal (Pietermaritzburg)

Photographs and sketches from: the KwaZulu-Natal
    Provincial Museum Service Collection

Lithographic repro by: 3 White Dogs

Contents

Anglo-Boer War Sites

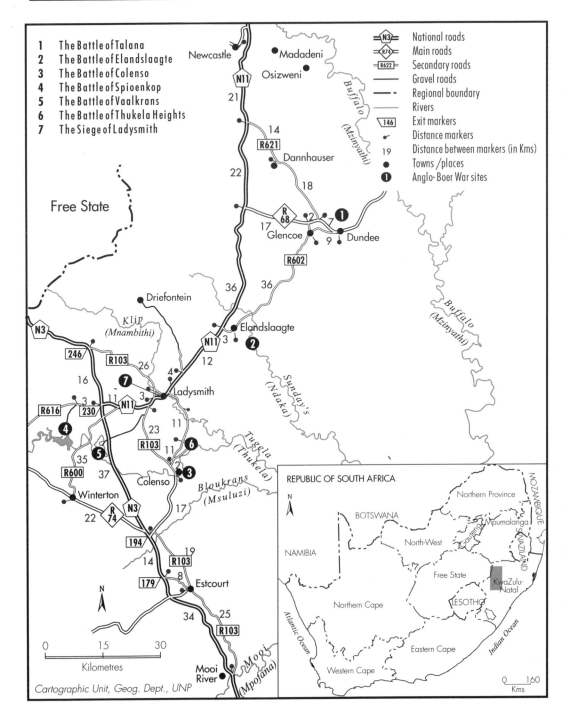

1 The Battle of Talana
2 The Battle of Elandslaagte
3 The Battle of Colenso
4 The Battle of Spioenkop
5 The Battle of Vaalkrans
6 The Battle of Thukela Heights
7 The Siege of Ladysmith

N3 National roads
R74 Main roads
R622 Secondary roads
Gravel roads
Regional boundary
Rivers
146 Exit markers
Distance markers
19 Distance between markers (in Kms)
Towns /places
1 Anglo- Boer War sites

Free State

Newcastle
Madadeni
Osizweni
N11
21
Buffalo (Mzinyathi)
R621
14
Dannhauser
22
18
R 68
17
Glencoe
2
7
1
9
Dundee
R602

36
36
Driefontein
Klip (Mnambithi)
N3
246
R103
26
4
12
N11
3
Elandslaagte
2
Sunday's (Naaka)
16
7
3
Ladysmith
R616
3
11
N11
230
11
23
11
R103
11
6
4
Tugela (Thukela)
5
35
2
3
R600
37
Colenso
Bloukrans (Msuluzi)
Winterton
17
22
R 74
N3
194
14
19
R103
179
8
Estcourt
N
34
25
R103
0   15   30
Kilometres
Mooi River
Mooi (Mpofana)
Cartographic Unit, Geog. Dept., UNP

REPUBLIC OF SOUTH AFRICA
N
BOTSWANA
Northern Province
MOZAMBIQUE
Gauteng
Mpumalanga
NAMIBIA
North-West
SWAZILAND
Free State
KwaZulu-Natal
Northern Cape
LESOTHO
Atlantic Ocean
Eastern Cape
Indian Ocean
Western Cape
0   160
Kms

Preface

This Battle Book series has been written to make information, photographs and maps of the most significant Anglo-Boer War sites in KwaZulu-Natal more readily available.

The books are not exhaustive studies of the various sites but rather field guides, designed to assist the reader in interpreting the terrain and understanding the events.

Although the Battle Books form a series, each book has been fully contextualised and can be followed on its own.

Contributors to this series share a long-term interest in the Anglo-Boer War and have each made their own unique contribution to the historiography and understanding of the conflict. With the assistance of an editorial committee, every effort has been made to maintain balance and accuracy.

A slightly flexible approach has been adopted to the spelling of names. As a general rule, the most recent spelling utilised on the state's Survey and Mapping 1:50 000 maps has been adopted. Thus for instance Laing's Nek becomes Lang's Nek. Where the name used to describe a topographical feature differs significantly from that in the historical literature to that appearing on the map, then the one used in the books and documents is adopted. The spelling of the river Thukela (Tugela) presents a slight problem. On the maps it is spelt as given in the brackets. However, in most current academic historical literature the former form has been adopted, which spelling has been followed in this series of books.

Introduction

At the outbreak of the Anglo-Boer War on 11 October 1899, Britain had 27 054 troops of all ranks, both imperial and colonial, deployed over a wide area of southern Africa. The major concentration of forces was in Natal, with Ladysmith as their base.

A detachment of 4 000 – 4 500 men, under the command of Major-General Sir William Penn Symons, had been sent forward to Dundee, arriving in the latter part of September. British military consensus held that the northern Natal triangle, vulnerable to attack from several points from across the Buffalo River and over the Drakensberg, should not be defended and the principal towns evacuated. However, a strong lobby, swayed by colonial mining interests, demanded the defence of Dundee and Elandslaagte; their mines were vital to the shipping companies. The British Government was relying on the shipping companies to transport men and materials from Britain and the

Major-General Sir William Penn Symons (1843 - 1899)

He was educated at Sandhurst and joined the 24th Regiment in 1863. He served with his regiment in a number of campaigns and saw service in many countries. He was involved in the Anglo-Zulu war in 1879 and wrote a report on the battle of Isandlwana. Shortly before the outbreak of the Anglo-Boer War he was posted to Natal with orders to take precautionary measures on the northern borders.

Empire. Moreover, rebellion by dissident Boers in the Biggarsberg and by disaffected Africans was a real threat. The decision was therefore taken to defend Dundee.

Symons was familiar with the area and its inhabitants. Twenty years earlier, after the disaster at Isandlwana, he had spent two months in Fort Jones, a sod fort which had been constructed on what was later to become part of the town of Dundee.

British intelligence relied on the Natal Scouts and Basuto guides. Their knowledge of the area and

A Boer commando in Newcastle on its way south into Natal.

that of Boer movements was excellent. Once the decision was made to defend Dundee and the British troops started arriving from 25 September onwards, Symons made special arrangements for the evacuation of the women and children from Dundee. Not all of them left, however, as they had been assured by Sir Harry Escombe, ex-Prime Minister of Natal, that there was no danger from the Boer forces. He was later to escape from Dundee dressed as a fat old lady on the post cart.

Asked what his plans were in case of attack, Symons asserted that he "had no plans but would be guided by circumstances". No attempt was made to picket the hills around Dundee, to prevent the Boer forces from occupying them. Dundee is surrounded by a ring of hills

Commandant-General Piet Joubert and staff having breakfast in Newcastle on 17 October 1899.

with Mpati Mountain – "the place of good waters" – being of strategic importance as it was the source of the town's water supply.

The military aims of the Boers were to neutralise the British forces threatening their sovereignty. They therefore decided to strike with significant numbers at the British forces, with the largest force focusing on Natal. The Boer leadership was expecting the biggest British attacks to come from Natal.

The biggest concentration of Boer commandos was therefore centred on the northern triangle of Natal. At various Drakensberg passes, mainly opposite Ladysmith, there were between 6 000 and 8 000 Orange Free State burghers. A little further north, at Botha's Pass, were the German Corps and Johannesburg Commando, numbering approximately 1 200 men. Still further north, near Volksrust, was the South African Republic's Commandant-General PJ Joubert with 10 000 to 12 000 burghers. At Wakkerstroom were the local commando and that from Ermelo, totalling 1 800 to 2 000 burghers and at Doringkop, opposite Dundee, lay the Utrecht, Vryheid and Piet Retief commandos, numbering between 1 500 and 2 000 burghers. The Boer force poised to enter northern Natal thus numbered between 20 500 and 25 200.

Once the Boers entered Natal they organised themselves into three columns. General Kock led the Johannesburg Commando and the Hollander and German Corps directly south over Mkupe Pass towards Elandslaagte Colliery and the railway station.

General D.J.E. "Maroela" Erasmus (1845 – 1914)
During the First Anglo-Boer war he was involved at Bronkhorstspruit and was wounded in a later engagement. He became commandant of the Pretoria commando and was a member of the Volksraad.

General DJE 'Maroela' Erasmus with 4 000 men from Pretoria, Heidelberg and Boksburg, moved south-east through Dannhauser and Hattingspruit. Swinging east, General Lucas Meyer led the Middelburg and Wakkerstroom commandos towards Utrecht and Vryheid to raise support in those areas. These two forces congregated at the Doornberg, the large flat mountain 19 kilometres to the north-east of Dundee, near the Blood River battlefield. Here they were led in prayer before advancing on Dundee. Their aim was to control the high areas around the town. Dietlof van Warmelo describes how he and the men with him moved from the Doornberg to occupy Mpati mountain:

"Before the commando started, a terrible thunderstorm came on that slowly passed over and was followed by gentle rain. We rode hard in the dark, through dongas, past farms and houses, zigzagging in a half-circle, to the mountains of Dundee... we had to await the dawn in the cold, drenched to the skin. A mackintosh is of small service in such rain. When the day dawned... a thick fog had come on. General Lucas Meyer was to begin the attack on the west, and we were to surprise the enemy from the heights."

'Maroela' Erasmus and his burgers were to hold Mpati mountain. Talana and Lennox (known also as little Talana) were to be occupied by Lucas Meyer and his 3 500 men.

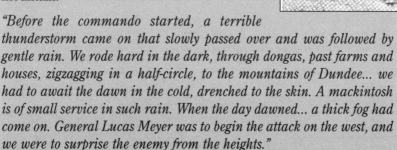

ERAAL LUCAS MEIJER

Lucas Meyer (1846 – 1902)

He grew up in Natal, settled in Utrecht and became a field cornet. He fought in the battle of Ingogo (1880) where he was wounded. He served as landdrost in Utrecht and with the formation of the New Republic became its president. When the New Republic merged with the ZAR he eventually became chairman of the Volksraad. At the outbreak of the war he held command in Natal as a general.

The first encounter

On Friday morning at 03:20 in the wet, inky darkness, Meyer's advance guard clashed with Lieutenant Grimshaw's picket some four kilometres beyond Smith's Nek, which is the saddle between Talana and Lennox hills, along the present road to Vryheid.

In this engagement the horses were stampeded, men wounded and the British picket forced to withdraw. A message to the British camp and Symons did not elicit any alarm. Symons believed this to be a raiding party, despite being warned the previous morning that an attack was imminent. It was only when a second message from Grimshaw was received to the effect that he and his men had taken up a new position in the bed of the Steenkoolspruit (also known as the Sandspruit) to prevent any further forward movement by the Boers that Symons sent out two infantry companies of the Royal Dublin Fusiliers in support.

By first light on the morning of the 20th the Boer forces had taken up their positions. On Talana Hill the commandos from Utrecht, Wakkerstroom, Krugersdorp, and a portion of the Ermelo commando, together with three guns (two Krupp 75mm and one Creusot 75mm) under Major Wolmarans of the Staats Artillerie were ready and waiting.

On Lennox Hill the commandos from Vryheid, Middelburg, Piet Retief and a few men from Bethal had taken up their position. Three guns were kept behind Lennox and were not used during the battle.

The start of the battle

At daybreak the tops of the hills were covered in swirling mist. In the British camp, life started as usual with the troops standing to at 05:00. At 05:20 they were dismissed to get breakfast, water the horses and start the usual camp fatigues (duties). As the mist slowly swirled away from the top of Talana Hill the troops in camp could clearly see figures silhouetted against the skyline. Were they the Town Guard, the men sent out during the night, or the Boers?

While waiting for signs of movement on Mpati mountain from 'Maroela' Erasmus, whose instructions were to support him in the

The members of the Dundee Town Guard and the Dundee Rifle Association who fought alongside the British forces in the battle of Talana.

attack, an anxious Lucas Meyer inspected the positions on Lennox. Erasmus' position on Mpati was some 335m higher than Talana and was covered in mist for much of the early morning. Meyer soon returned to the top of Talana where the men were urging him to give them permission to "say good morning to the British". Meyer eventually gave permission for the first shells to be fired. The Boers soon found the range, with their second shell landing near the entrance to Symons's tent. It failed to explode as it buried itself in the damp ground. It was now about 05:40.

Although confusion reigned briefly in the British camp, discipline and training soon prevailed. The 67th artillery battery immediately opened fire on Talana Hill but at 3 230

The terrain over which the British troops advanced to attack the Boers on Talana Hill. Also visible is the plantation they passed through and the last stone wall along the upper terrace.

metres distant it was slightly out of range. Within 15 minutes the 69th and 13th batteries had limbered up and advanced to a knoll just south of the town from where they promptly opened fire on Talana Hill. Gunner Netley recorded his impression of the rapid movement through the town where the civilians were "supplying the men with coffee and cocoa, also some bread and butter, which comes very acceptable indeed". The British bombardment of the hilltop was accurate. "Talana se kruin het 'n ware hel van barstende bomme en vliegende klipsplinters geword." (The crown of Talana Hill became a hell of bursting bombs and flying rock splinters.) Major Wolmarans withdrew his guns from the forward slopes of the hill to safety and thus they took no further part in the battle.

Symons immediately issued orders for the attack by ordering a frontal assault on Talana Hill. The Royal Dublin Fusiliers and the Royal Irish

Fusiliers were to advance to the Steenkoolspruit with the King's Royal Rifles in support. The 1st Leicestershire, the 67th artillery battery, the Natal Police and the company of the Natal Carbineers were left to defend the camp in case of attack from the rear. Lieutenant-Colonel Möller with the 18th Hussars and Mounted Infantry was sent out behind Talana Hill. They moved off towards the gap between Mpati and Talana to try to cut off any retreat by the Boers.

Members of the Dundee Town Guard and the Rifle Association joined the Royal Dublin Fusiliers as they moved through the town. On Talana Hill the big guns were no longer returning the British fire and Lucas Meyer was waiting for Erasmus on Mpati to make a move and so force the British to change the direction of their attack. Erasmus made no attempt at any stage in the attack on Talana Hill to assist Meyer. His only action was to send men to capture Möller and his mounted men. Deneys Reitz, one of the men on Mpati mountain, recorded his feelings in his book *Commando*,

"When it grew light the rain ceased, but a mist enshrouded the mountain-top through which everything looked ghostly and uncertain... and when Maroela was asked for orders he merely stood glowering into the fog without reply... towards midday the weather cleared somewhat, and while it still continued misty, patches of sunshine began to splash the plain...And then, far down, into one of these sunlit patches rode a troop of English horsemen about 300 strong. This was our first sight of the enemy, and we followed their course with close attention."

Symons came down to the Steenkoolspruit to give instructions for the advance to begin. The plan of attack was slightly changed as the Dublin Fusiliers and the King's Royal Rifles would lead the attack with the Irish Fusiliers in support. At 07:20 the right-hand company of the

British troops advancing up the lower slopes of Talana Hill.

Dublin Fusiliers emerged in open order from the spruit and started running for Smith's farm some 700 – 900 metres away. They were closely followed by the King's Royal Rifles. Meanwhile some of the Boers had moved down from the crest of the hill to

Indian stretcher bearers operated from the medical station on the banks of the Steenkoolspruit. Talana was the first battle in which, under enemy fire, they moved about the battlefield rescuing the wounded British soldiers and took them to medical posts, and then on to the temporary hospitals which had been set up.

the plateau to ensure that the advancing British troops were within range of their Mauser rifles. As the British advanced across the open plain to the cover of some blue gum trees, an unlucky few were hit by long-range rifle fire. The fire was intense, but at extreme range it was not that effective. In a patch of corn close to the river, the Indian dhoolie bearers (stretcher bearers) found their first casualties.

Gallantly they carried them off the battlefield time after time, under heavy rifle fire, to Betania, the Cottage Hospital and other buildings being used as hospitals throughout the town. In a letter to his father, Sergeant Arthur Harrington recorded how,

"Never shall I forget the dreadful storm of bullets that smote us those awful moments. Exposed to a crossfire from thousands of rifles, men commenced to fall rapidly, whilst the air and ground all around us were torn by the fearful hail ... To my joy, however, the edge of the wood was at length reached, and by great good luck it was just where there was a little bit of wall, behind which I dropped, and had barely done so when two bullets struck the uppermost stones."

The British took cover in the gum tree plantations around Smith's farm and one of the distinctive memories of the battle was the smell of eucalyptus as the gum trees were stripped bare by the Boer rifle fire. In the plantation they sought what cover they could find. In the process the units became jumbled up. Some of the King's Royal Rifles and the Irish Fusiliers moved to their right to reply to heavy fire coming from Lennox Hill. Most of the Dublin Fusiliers meanwhile made their way to the left, to a deep, winding donga (dry gully) which ran up the hillside. It seemed to offer good cover from fire from the top of Talana. The remainder of the British force had penetrated to the front of the plantation. Several Boers had in the meantime come off the summit on to a lower terrace from where they were mounting a searching and trying attack.

By 08:00 the British artillery had moved to a position along the Steenkoolspruit and were now somewhat closer to the action. They concentrated their fire on Talana. Brigadier-General Yule realised the futility of a frontal attack and allowed the men to seek what cover they could and for a while there was no further movement.

The British advance on Talana Hill.

By 09:00 Symons had become impatient as the attack was still static. He rode on to the battlefield to encourage the troops and order them up the hill.

Despite requests from his officers to either take cover, retire from the field or dismiss the trooper who was carrying the penant, he moved forward relentlessly. At the first stone wall, just at the edge of the trees around Smith's farm, he was shot in the stomach. He handed over the command to Yule and retired from the field. The military surgeon pronounced his wound fatal. He died two days later and is buried in St James Anglican churchyard in Dundee.

Major-General Sir William Penn Symons was mortally wounded during the battle of Talana. He was on foot when the incident took place and this sketch is therefore inaccurate. When the bullet struck Symons he said to Major Murray who was with him, "I am severely, mortally, wounded in the stomach".

The attack up the hill

Yule now gave the order to storm the hill and take their second objective – the stone wall at the edge of the plateau. The Dublin Fusiliers were to make their way to the upper wall on the left, while the King's Royal Rifles, supported by two companies of the Irish Fusiliers, were to advance on the right. On the left, progress was difficult as the donga the Dublin Fusiliers used for cover soon petered out. Directly in front of the plantation the terrain was more favourable for the British infantry. For about 100 metres there was a fairly level terrace which was swept by rifle fire from a range of 550 metres. Beyond it, however, the ground rose steeply to a stone wall. This steep slope gave complete cover from fire from above and also to a degree from the flank. A low stone wall, on the right running from top to bottom of the hill, also provided cover against the flanking fire.

An attempt was made by the Dublin Fusiliers to move up the donga on the left flank of the hill. They hoped that this would provide them with cover and it appeared to come out at the plateau. However, it did not provide the shelter and coverage expected as it became narrower and shallower as it rose up the hill. Towards the top of the donga the troops were met by intense rifle fire as the Boers had been watching their movements all the way. It was at the top of this donga that many of the officers lost their lives. The Dublin Fusiliers' advance was checked.

In the centre the King's Royal Rifles and two companies of Irish Fusiliers were ordered to advance. First they had to negotiate a dense hedge and beyond it the 100 metre wide open terrace. As they emerged on to this they came under fierce fire. Soon men were falling, dead or wounded on the open ground. Others dashed forward, lost heart, and ran back to cover. Others, however, made it safely to the bottom of the steep slope and cover. The officers led these men up the slope and to the stone wall running along the top of it. There they spread out under its cover. Some of the men left in the plantation braced themselves and again pushed forward, many making use of the cross wall for cover.

Few casualties resulted as these additional men pushed forward. At the wall casualties did, however, continue to mount. The King's Royal Rifles attempted to return the fire. To show oneself above the stone wall was to brave the storm of a dozen rifles. Colour Sergeant Clarke recalled how "it was instant death" to move from the protection offered by the stone wall and how he was instructed to

> "... Put your helmet up slowly and see if it draws fire. I raised it on the end of my rifle and it was shattered by a hurricane of bullets... After a short while I raised what was left of my helmet, but this time, strangely, there was no fire drawn, so I shouted to my comrades to advance and a few men followed me... I turned and shouted to the Dublins to come on."

On top of Talana Hill, Lucas Meyer continually tried to heliograph Erasmus on Mpati, but received no response. His supply of ammunition was running low, his men were exhausted, his position was becoming tenuous and as there was still no sign of Erasmus entering the fight he gave the signal to his men to start withdrawing from the hill and to regroup at the Doornberg. A small number of men would remain to protect this withdrawal. The Boer rifle fire became less intense. It was now about 11:30.

The battlefield as seen from the top stone wall. Also visible is the stone wall which went from top to bottom and behind which the British sheltered from fire from Lennox Hill while advancing up Talana Hill.

Colonel Gunning of the King's Royal Rifles believed the time had come for the final charge. In front of them lay about 50 metres of open, flat ground and then a steep slope embedded with large rocks, covered by tall grass and bushes. The artillery, which by now was no more than 1 400 metres from the Talana summit, was signalled to cease firing. Then came the shout from Gunning, "Advance!". The British troops rushed across the plateau, making a dash for the base of the steep slope. They were again met by a furious hail of rifle fire from the few Boers who were positioned along the crest of the hill. The artillery decided to clear the Boers off the hillside and started bombarding the top of the hill and the plateau again. This bombardment also cleared the plateau area of their own men, who were forced to take cover from the shrapnel from their own guns. It was imperative to draw the attention of the gunners to their plight. Signaller Private Flynn of the Royal Dublin Fusiliers jumped up and exposed himself to rifle fire in an attempt to "call up" the guns. After repeated unsuccessful attempts he dashed down the hillside to deliver the message personally. When questioned about firing on their own men the answer was that as the British troops were wearing khaki uniforms it was extremely difficult to distinguish between friend and foe. Furthermore, they were aiming at the plateau which was where Boer riflemen had been in position earlier in the morning.

Captain Weldon - Royal Dublin Fusiliers - was the first British officer killed in the war. During the battle of Talana his servant, Private Cotty was wounded and in rushing to his aid, Weldon was killed. His body was found the following day because his terrier, 'Rose', was sitting whining next to it. He is buried in the cemetery at Talana museum.

Immediately after this bombardment the British troops stormed the hill, clambering up the last rock-strewn vertical section to reach the top. Once they had started moving up the vertical face it did provide some relief from the Boer rifle fire as they were protected by the hill.

Viewing the battlefield. The Boer perspective from the top of Talana Hill.

The Boer withdrawal

Lucas Meyer had started moving burghers off the hilltop, sending them back across the Natal border. The resistance was not as stiff as it had been and the British troops finally made it to the top of the hill. By 14:00 the entire position was in British hands. The artillery batteries were brought up into Smith's Nek but did not fire on the withdrawing Boers. No one will ever know the reason why – it has been said that Colonel Pickwoad saw a white flag flying and sent to Yule for instructions before opening fire. It has also been suggested that he believed some of the mounted men in greatcoats to be the 18th Hussars and was reluctant to open fire on British troops again. The men on the hill also stopped firing as the the bugle announcing "all clear" sounded across the hilltop. When some of the men believed this to be a mistake and commenced firing on the withdrawing Boers, the "all clear" sounded once again. Thus the Boer force rode off northwards under the eyes of the British and no attempt was made to stop them. Late that afternoon, with the Dundee Town Guard manning Talana Hill, the British troops returned to their camp along the streets lined with cheering townspeople.

Certainly the Boers were withdrawing towards the Buffalo River and their forces were temporarily demoralised, but they had been saved from suffering serious losses by the failure of the artillery batteries on Smith's Nek to fire on them. The commandos crossed the Buffalo River unscathed.

Moving to and fro across the battlefield the entire time, were the Indian stretcher bearers. They carried the wounded off to the field dressing stations and into the town to the temporary hospitals which had been set up. These stretcher bearer corps were raised in both South Africa and India to serve as non-combatant medical personnel. Volunteers from local Indians in the town also assisted during the battle. The front verandahs of the two Smith homesteads, at the base of Talana Hill, were used as field dressing stations.

The capture of the cavalry

Möller and the cavalry had earlier in the day taken up a position behind Talana Hill. Major Knox and a detachment of men had been sent off to scout behind Lennox Hill. They surprised a small group of Boers and managed to disperse them, taking a number of prisoners, who were sent back to Möller. Later that day when he was captured these Boers were released.

With the Boer forces moving northwards to the Transvaal border, Möller had found his small group of men directly in the path of the Boer commandos. He quickly realised that he was not dealing with a defeated army but one well able to cope with his small group of cavalry and he therefore retreated in a northerly direction, as he realised that he could do nothing to prevent the Boer withdrawal. He attempted to recall Knox but could not get a message to him because of the large numbers of Boers between them.

A group of Boers made a determined attack on the mounted infantry who were part of Möller's force. The cavalry were forced to fall back with the mounted infantry covering their retreat. In these skirmishes the Boers captured a Maxim, which had got stuck in a spruit. Lieutenant Cape rendered it useless by destroying the water-jacket. Möller's men moving at a gallop followed him across the Sandspruit towards the northern extremity of Mpati. At first he apparently moved in this direction by mistake as he believed it to be the direction from which they had moved out of the town. After realising his mistake he was unwilling to retrace his steps for fear of being cut off by the Boers and decided to return to the camp by a route around Mpati mountain and towards Glencoe. When he got abreast of Mpati mountain he was spotted by the Boer forces on the top.

> "The Colonel trusted in getting safely back round by the Navigation Collieries... Our luck, however, was dead out... My advance scout reported the presence of Boers... and I soon observed parties of them descending the slopes of Impati. It was now clear that to push on in the direction we were taking was but to court disaster. We were heading for a new commando, one which had taken no part in the battle. Thereupon the Colonel decided on taking up as strong a position as could be found handy and holding out to nightfall in the hope of slipping away in the dark."

A force of some 100 burghers under Commandant Trichardt cut them off from further movement around Mpati mountain. Möller and his men took up a defensive position on Adelaide farm. The buildings of Maritz's farm seemed to offer the best chance for defence until nightfall when they could slip away back to Dundee. The Hussars took up a position in the barn, while the mounted infantry were on a slight knoll about 180 metres away. At first they were able to hold their own but a Maxim gun was brought up shortly after 15:00. The shells from this gun stampeded the horses, and the British found they were running short of ammunition. Just after 16:30 Möller decided to surrender. Their losses were eight killed, 18 wounded and 209 taken prisoner-of-war. Major Knox and the rest of the Hussars worked their way back to camp, arriving at about 19:00 in the evening.

The stone cairn which marks the spot where General Symons fell mortally wounded during the battle.

Counting the cost

With the battle over the British counted their losses: 51 men killed, 203 wounded and 246 taken prisoner of war – a total of 500 men. The Boer casualties were much lighter, the estimated figures of their losses being 30 – 40 killed, 100 – 120 wounded and 12 taken prisoner of war – a total of between 142 and 172.

However, the question remains – who won the battle of Talana? The British troops had driven Lucas Meyer and his men off both Talana and Lennox – but the Boers were by no means a defeated army. At first glance it appears as though the British won the battle. However, within 30 hours they were forced to abandon the town and retreat to Ladysmith. They left behind their unburied dead and their wounded who became prisoners-of-war. The Boer officers ordered the Indians to bury the British dead, several of whom were already decomposing. Stores and ammunition were looted by the Boers, who occupied the town for the next seven months, renaming it Meyersdorp in honour of Lucas Meyer.

Talana may not rank as a major battle in terms of the total numbers engaged but it had a significant moral effect. It was the first battle of the war and it appeared as though the impact of Majuba had been reversed. The news of the battle spread rapidly throughout South Africa with far-reaching effects.

The Boer forces formed an entirely different impression of the British soldier. He was far braver and more determined than they had been led to believe. The British soldier also realised that the Boers, although an irregular army, would prove to be a formidable foe.

The first battle of the Anglo-Boer War had come to an end, in what proved to be a long and bitter conflict. With hindsight it is unlikely that this battle would have been fought, but for political reasons. Dundee, like Newcastle, would have been evacuated and left to the Boer forces were it not for influential men and their coal mining interests.

Yule realised that he was unable to defend Dundee and decided to withdraw to Ladysmith. Reconnaissance exercises had revealed large concentrations of Boers in the Glencoe area, making retreat along the railway line impossible. The only alternative was the Helpmekaar road to Beith, down Van Tonder's Pass and across the Sunday's River to Ladysmith.

At 21:00 on Sunday 22 October, the Army Service Corps moved the wagons into camp to load the four days' worth of supplies that the retreating troops would need. By midnight, they were moving quietly out of the camp, leaving lighted candles in the tents and fires burning to create the illusion that the camp was occupied.

The Boers only discovered that the British had left on Monday morning. They assumed that the British would have taken the railway route and followed the tracks for some distance before realising that this was not so. They also wasted time by looting Dundee before setting out in pursuit of the British.

A copy from the page of the Town Clerk's letter book. Burkett wrote this message before leading the civilians of Dundee out of the town to march with the British forces to Ladysmith.

Brigadier-General Yule's retreating column making its way back to Ladysmith.

The British retreat proved to be a long, exhausting and fearful march to Ladysmith for the British troops. The first halt was allowed on Monday afternoon, but this was very brief as they were afraid of pursuit and capture by the Boers. The descent of Van Tonder's Pass took place in pitch darkness and pouring rain. It was a very trying time as not only was it muddy and slippery, but there was constant fear of ambush. The descent took from 21:30 until 03:00. In the early hours of Tuesday as the troops were marching towards the Sunday's River, they were joined by the Dundee citizens who had left the town under the guidance of the town clerk. They had quickly packed a few belongings and left the town following the route over Wenkommando Pass to join the British troops. Some of the Indian families who had not already left the town marched with this group to Ladysmith.

By 09:30 on Tuesday morning the British forces, having crossed bad roads in the dark and now joined by the Dundee citizens, had crossed the Wasbank river. On Wednesday they reached the Sunday's River and waited for an escort of the 5th Lancers who had been sent out from Ladysmith to meet them. That evening, the last stretch – an arduous twelve-hour night march to Ladysmith – began. At 06:00 on Thursday morning, 26 October they reached Ladysmith. The troops were exhausted, caked with mud, soaking wet and very hungry, but they had not straggled and had not lost a single person on the retreat.

It had taken 81 hours to retreat from Dundee to Ladysmith. The men had been on their feet for 40 of those hours. The average pace of the 3.2 kilometre (2 mile) long column was 2.5 kilometres (1.5 miles) per hour.

A colliery manager from Dundee recorded his feelings:

"We were dead tired, and hungry, and footsore, but we went on until four in the morning, and then we knew we were retreating on Ladysmith. I cannot go into the awful hardships we encountered, walking seventy miles in horrible storms of rain and thunder. Suffice to say, we walked for five days with not a dry thread on us, and nothing to eat except hard biscuits and bully beef. The last mile I walked without boots; they had fallen off my feet."

After the war – A peaceful picnic for General Lucas Meyer, his wife and friends on the battlefield of Talana Hill.

Conclusion

The Commandant-General blamed the failure to cut off and capture Yule's force while still in Dundee, on the weather and the lack of co-ordination among the Boer officers. The weather continued to be inclement in the days following the battle, with mist and drizzle about. Meanwhile, Commandant Weilbach of the Heidelberg commando refused to co-operate with Erasmus and made himself so unpleasant that only one of his veld-cornets supported him. Jannie Smuts, the Zuid-Afrikaansche Republiek state attorney, also reported that there was inadequate organisation and no proper tactical plan. These were all hallmarks of a non-professional army.

There was very little to stop the Boers from moving south once they had control of Dundee and from there could have challenged Lieutenant-General Sir George White for the overall control of northern Natal.

Dundee under occupation

The Reverend Gerard Chilton Bailey, Anglican Vicar to the parish of St James, remained in Dundee during the entire Boer occupation, from 23 October 1899 – 6 May 1900, despite numerous attempts by the Boer authorities to remove him to Pretoria. During this time he kept a diary, extracts of which are reproduced below.

His dry wit and ability to accurately describe events and scenes, make this diary extremely interesting to read – it is almost as though the reader is standing behind a curtained window detachedly watching events pass by.

With his camera, he took numerous snap-shots. For safety, he placed his camera "into the bookseller's store. On the following Monday, when the Boers occupied the town, they wrecked the store and I have not seen my camera again". What a pity, as the list of photographs (which is thoughtfully provided) would have added greatly to the record of the battle of Talana.

On October 23rd, he records the following:

"My birthday and I shall not forget it in a hurry. The troops had left Dundee, but where for, nobody knew. All the wounded – nearly 200 – and the Field Hospitals, were left behind. The best part of the Town Guard and many of the residents had gone with the troops. Other residents had left the town, some on foot, some on horseback for Greytown or the railway south of Ladysmith. More hurried away during the morning. I think it would be about 10 o'clock that I went into a store. The owner told me he was just off. I remember I secured a large piece of bacon, and as much bread as I could carry, besides other eatables. There was no knowing how we should be fixed. One

---

thing was certain; the Boers would before long occupy the town. About 11 the Resident Magistrate released 17 Boer prisoners, who were in the town goal. They gave their word that they would not take up arms again against the British. A little later a Boer brought in the following letter to the Magistrate. It was in Dutch.

'To the Magistrate or other official entrusted with the civil administration of Dundee.

Dear Sir,

Unless you, sir hand over the town of Dundee before or by 2 o'clock this afternoon, I will treat the above mentioned town as I think fit and bombard the same.

I remain,

   Your, &c.

23.10.99 D. Erasmus

   (Asst. General)'

There of course could only be one answer. Such are the fortunes of war! In all my letters to England I had up to the last, declared that Dundee was as safe as the bank of England, and here we are, surrendered to the enemy".

The Boer forces, after entering the town, immediately began looting – all stores and offices came in for the same treatment. "The only two that successfully resisted the looters, were Messrs Oldacres and Handley's, and these only to a limited extent, as later on they were taken over by the Transvaal authorities and then the looting was done in a more genteel manner. The Boer in his looting had his own particular fancies.

Macintoshes were eagerly snapped up. Sardines were never passed over, and Dutch Bibles were taken as Godsends. I found one Boer gloating over a heavy, well bound one. 'Hullo, got a bible?' I said. His eyes beamed with satisfaction. Most of the Boers went for new garments. One could hardly blame them for this prudence, as there was plenty of roughing in store for them."

On November 2, a notice ordering all inhabitants resident in a 3 mile radius to report to the railway station for transport to Pretoria, was issued.

"Should it be true that we are to be sent to Pretoria, it was necessary that I should hide away all plate, china, and valuables from the looting of the Natal Dutch. First I spent an hour under the house burrowing like a rabbit, and feeling very much, I expect, as a miner does, in a three foot seam of coal. I did not proceed with this for very long, as it suddenly struck me that the Church was safer than the house and that there was a roomy basement below the flooring. The walk up the nave of the Church is covered with linoleum, and I had only to raise this and saw out two boards and tack down the linoleum again. All I had in the way of tools were a broken chisel, a large saw and a hammer. The latter I dared not use much, as there were now Boer Policemen patrolling, and the Church stands between two roads. The using of a light was another difficulty. A bright idea struck me – I would use my ruby photographic lamp! And as the windows of the Church are coloured and pretty thick glass too, I felt that my light would not betray me. I lit the lamp and went outside to have a look; there was no sign of any light from the windows, a professional burglar could not have done better, except that he would have brought an awl and a narrow saw. However, I chiselled away and taking a blow with a hammer every two minutes or so, I got through the wood, and then the sawing was soon done. Father M helped me to pack together the plate and co, in various small bundles, and the conveyance of them over to the Church I left till early morning. I was up about 4.30 am – again a burglaring. I dug several holes in the garden and buried the china and co, (afterwards planting potatoes over them). I next put on my MA gown having folds capacious enough to conceal packages, and started making journeys to and from the Church. I had not been over

Members of the Boer occupation force in Dundee in front of the town buildings. The Zuid-Arikaansche Republiek flag is flying over the building.

many times and was venturing across with a handbag well-filled, when I saw a Boer guard with Mauser cocked bearing down upon me. He called me to him and asked me what I was up to. I said 'I am the predikant (minister) of this Church!' and he at once beamed on me and uncocked his Mauser and warned me to make my house 'very nice' and 'stoppee the doors', and so on. He walked into the Vicarage and at once started locking all the doors. He told me he was a Dutchman from the old Colony (Cape colony) but no more British rule for him! It was 'very hard' he could earn 25/- a day in

Johannesburg, and now he only got £2 a week for being a policeman. And then he cursed the English up hill and down dale. His language was very broken, but his oaths were English and so I understood what he was driving at. I wished him 'good bye' in the friendliest manner possible – he was an uncommon pleasant fellow — and went on with my work, rather pleased with the encounter, for he was the guard for this part of the town, and I was well known to him and quite above suspicion, with no fear of espionage. I soon finished my operations and when I had replaced the boards and linoleum, I walked up and down the aisle feeling I had set the wily Dutchman a poser this time, but I must not boast as I am not out the wood yet."

The Rev Bailey managed to keep up his good humour despite all privations and fears and his attempts to wash his clothes, are most amusing.

"Yesterday I successfully washed some flannel shirts, but collars are beyond me. This is awkward as I consider my clerical collar as a distinct mark for safety, the enemy having great respect for the cloth. NB. I afterwards found some starch and irons, and literally astonished myself. The collars were not very stiff but distinctly wearable. I put one on, and a wounded officer said that I was the best dressed man he had seen in the hospital."

Life went on under occupation after the Rev Bailey and Murray had managed to talk the Boer Kommandant into allowing them to stay in Dundee. On 17 November he records that "The Boer population in Dundee is being added to daily. Many fresh families have arrived. They are making themselves comfortable in the houses, and appear to have made up their

minds that this is to be a Boer dorp now and always. Henceforth it is to be 'Meyersdorp', named after Lucas Meyer."

On November 20 "A novel military punishment was inflicted today. For being out of bounds, an orderly of the hospital was sentenced to 21 days in bed."

On November 28 "An official arrived this morning with a pot of 'stickphast' and some slips of paper, with numbers very indifferently inscribed. He ticketed me with 37, which he stuck on the verandah post. My address is now 37 'Meyersdorp', Natal, SAR. I am described as chaplain to the hospital. The said label did not stick long; rain came and washed it off."

After some hard times with very little news of the outside world, and that which he did receive being exaggerated and very little food except the vegetables he grew and the chickens he managed to keep, on 5 February he records "Oldacre's and Handley's store are open again. I went to see what there was. Practically no provisions, but hunting in the back room I came across a box of tinned salmon (Lazenby's) and some soap. I wanted a pair of shoes. I found all leather were in a hopeless jumble. There seemed to be no pairs. After an hour's search I had to content myself with a pair – lady's – large size, for which I paid 6/6."

On 11 February he records "At the commencement of the occupation they talked about giving Dundee the new name of Meyersdorp. I saw an envelope so addressed; but now they have gone a step further, and are in reality renaming the streets. I saw yesterday near the gaol and Court House some erections which I thought were sign posts, directing strangers to these public buildings, but on going to examine I found on them inscribed 'General Joubert Straat', (street between Vicarage and gaol) 'Reitz Straat' (street past Willson's house, Handley's house and on to cemetery), 'President Kruger Straat' (Main Street), 'Wolmarans Straat' (street from market place to Hogo's house). All this tickled my fancy so much, that when I came upon the sign posts for the first time, I had a laughing fit in the street. Fancy this move, and the next town Ladysmith, not yet in their hands – rather premature! These signboards were after the relief of Ladysmith, stealthily removed."

Entertainment was provided by "What I call the Dundee Band performed this evening. One of the enemy who occupies a house near at hand plays a concertina uncommonly well. It has been a lovely moonlight night, and I have been sitting out on the verandah, thinking of the good times coming and listening to the strains of music. He has given us this evening: 'Wait till the clouds roll by', 'When the war is over we'll part no more', 'The keel row', 'Sweet Dreamland faces', 'Now the day is over', 'There is a boarding school, not far away', 'Rule Britannia'(!), and 'Home, Sweet Home'. Most of them most appropriate. I fancy he does not know the names and significance of all his tunes."

On March 2 he records that "This had been a distinctly cheery day. As I lay in bed at 5 am I was roused by a heavy report which shook the house. I knew at once the meaning of it. It told of the Boer retreat, and blowing up the bridges. Another, half an hour later, and then another. I am told that other explosions were heard earlier, but they did not

Furniture looted by Boers from the town's homes lying in the street in Dundee.

disturb me. This is indeed a good business. At midday a train full of Boer families, late residents of Dundee, steamed away. A distinctly good sign for the Boer women are far from desirous of quitting their comfortable abodes. Most of them had never had such a good time in their lives. You can be sure they are not going away empty, and I doubt if any Dundee housewives will ever set eyes upon their stocks of linen and the clothes they left behind."

His diary continues to record the movement of Boer Commando groups through the town and the retreat of those from Ladysmith, but on 15 May he is able to record joyously and with tremendous relief "Relieved! again safe and sound under British rule! I had a fitful night as far as sleep goes. I kept thinking that I might not be awake sufficiently early, and I was very anxious to hoist the British flag directly any of our troops came in sight. I had a small tree cut down the previous day for a flagstaff and was soon fastening to it the flag I had had in hiding for the last 7 months. Seven months yesterday since that same flag had served as General Penn-Symon's shroud. A hole was dug just behind the General's grave ready for the flag-staff. I was eager to hoist aloft, but I thought it wiser to be cautious and abide aweel. There was no knowing where the wily Boer might be hiding. At 7 o'clock a spider and a couple of horses came along toward the Church. It was the last of the Boers. I recognised a telegraph clerk; he pulled up. I bade him goodbye, and wished him luck.

About 8.30 my coloured gardener came rushing up. He had seen 3 soldiers. 'Up with the flag then'. There wasn't a breath of wind, not a breeze for her to wave to. Quite disappointing; but there she was, aloft and proud, the supreme symbol of our freedom, the end of the weary waiting, and well worth waiting for. Not many minutes had passed before I was shaking hands with the first man to enter Dundee."

One of his final comments, was that he would not have missed the seven months of occupation "For a good deal".

Forces engaged

Boer forces

Commanding officer: General Lucas Meyer

Utrecht commando (Commandant Joshua Joubert - 775 men)

Wakkerstroom commando (Commandant Hattingh - 713 men)

Krugersdorp commando (Commandant Potgieter - 860 men)

Portion of the Ermelo commando

Transvaal Staats Artillerie (Major Wolmarans)

Vryheid commando (Commandant Ferriera - 944 men)

Middelburg commando (Commandant Trichardt - 769 men)

Piet Retief commando (Commandant Engelbrecht - 432 men)

Portion of commando from Bethal (Commandant Greyling)

Total strength about 3 500 men.

Artillery

Two 75mm Krupp

One 75mm Creusot

3 other guns kept behind Lennox and not used.

British forces

Commanding Officer: Major-General Sir William Penn Symons
2nd Royal Dublin Fusiliers (Major Bird)
1st Royal Irish Fusiliers
1st Kings Royal Rifles (Lieutenant-Colonel Gunning)
1st Leicestershire Regiment
18th Hussars   (Colonel Möller)

Artillery
67th Artillery battery
69th Artillery battery
13th Artillery battery

4 363 men
1 568 horses
18 field guns

Colonial forces

Natal Police
Natal Carbineers
Dundee Town Guard
Dundee Rifle Association

Losses

	British	Boers
Killed	52 (including 10 officers)	31 (1 officer)
Wounded	203 (including 20 officers)	66
POW	246 (including 9 officers)	20

The battlefield today

The battlefield today forms part of the Talana Museum complex, on the outskirts of Dundee. Drive through Dundee on the R33 towards Vryheid. The museum covers 20 acres with a variety of displays in ten different historical buildings. The military conflicts of 1838, 1879, 1899 – 1902 form one of the sections. The national Consol glass museum, the national coal mine museums and other displays relevant to the Dundee area form part of the complex. Extensive archive facilities on the military history, coal mining and local events are available for researchers.

Visiting hours:

Weekdays 08:00 - 16:30
Saturdays 10:00 - 16:30
Sundays/Public holidays 12:00 - 16:30
Private Bag 2024, Dundee 3000
Tel 0341-22654
Fax 0341-22376

On battlefield site:

Museum, restaurant, tea garden, curio shop, picnic and braai facilities, conference venue, historical hiking trail, British forts, Boer and British gun emplacements.
Nominal entrance fee payable.
Daily tours to surrounding battlefields by registered
battlefield guides.

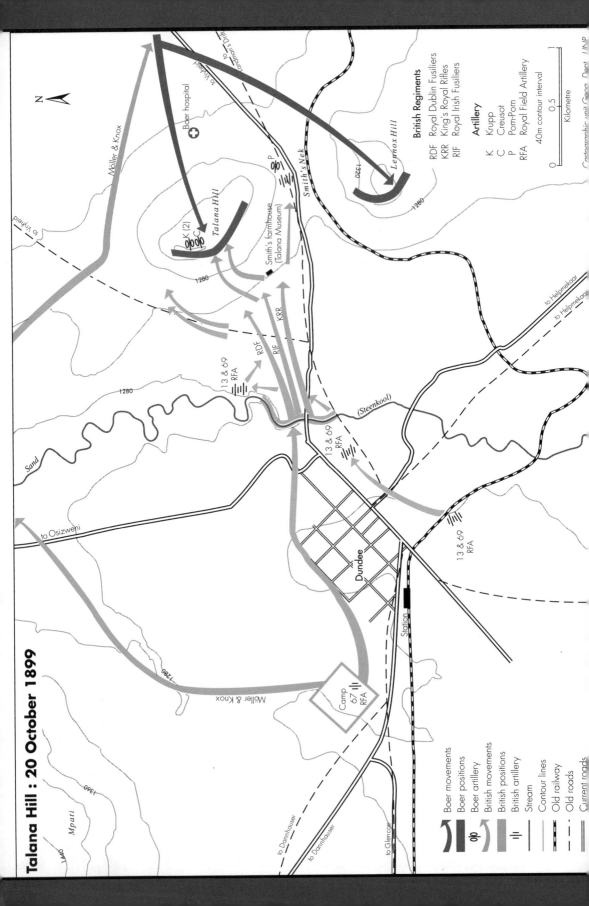

Talana Hill : 20 October 1899

British Regiments
RDF Royal Dublin Fusiliers
KRR King's Royal Rifles
RIF Royal Irish Fusiliers

Artillery
K Krupp
C Creusot
P Pom-Pom
RFA Royal Field Artillery

40m contour interval

0   0.5   Kilometre

Cartographic unit, Geog. Dept. UNP

Boer hospital

Talana Hill

K (2)

Smith's farmhouse
(Talana Museum)

Lennox Hill

1320

1280

Smith's Nek

Möller & Knox

to Vryheid

to Gardiner's Drift

to Vryheid

13 & 69 RFA

RDF

RIF

KRR

13 & 69 RFA

(Steenkool)

Sand

to Osizweni

Dundee

Station

Camp
67 RFA

Möller & Knox

1280

1280

1280

1360

Mpati

1440

to Dannhauser

to Dannhauser

to Glencoe

to Helpmekaar

to Helpmekaar

Boer movements
Boer positions
Boer artillery
British movements
British positions
British artillery
Stream
Contour lines
Old railway
Old roads
Current roads

N

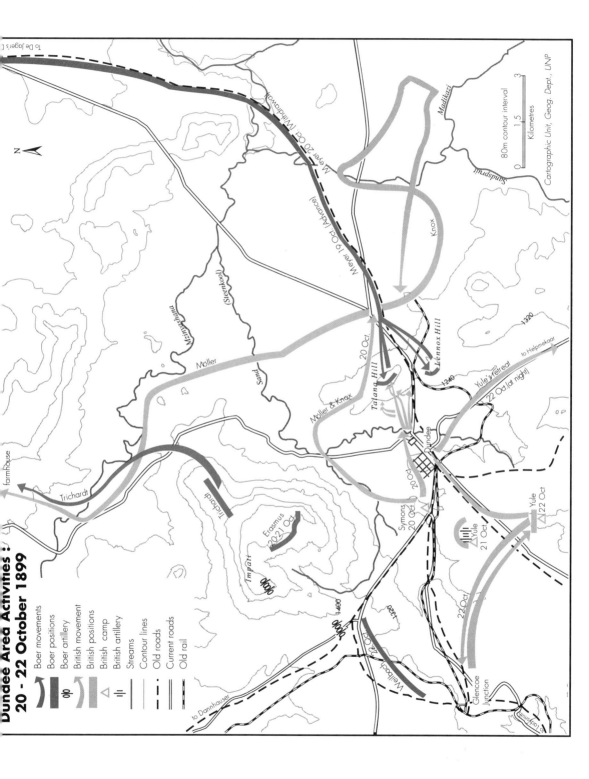

Dundee Area Activities :
20 - 22 October 1899

Boer movements
Boer positions
Boer artillery
British movement
British positions
British camp
British artillery
Streams
Contour lines
Old roads
Current roads
Old rail

80m contour interval

Kilometres
0   1.5   3

Cartographic Unit, Geog. Dept., UNP

N

To De Jager's D...

Meyer 20 Oct. (Withdrawal)

Meyer 19 Oct. (Advance)

20 Oct.

Madikazi

Sandspruit

Knox

Lennox Hill

1320

1240

Talang Hill

Möller & Knox

to Helpmekaar

Yule's retreat

22 Oct (at night)

Dundee

20 Oct.

20 Oct.

Symons, 20 Oct.

Yule 22 Oct

Yule 21 Oct

22 Oct

(Steenkool)

Mtintyathana

Möller

Sand

Trichardt

farmhouse

Trichardt

Erasmus 20-21 Oct

Impati

1400

1320

Weilbach 22 Oct

to Dannhauser

Glencoe Junction

to Ladysmith

43

Additional reading

Amery, L.S. *The Times History of the War in South Africa* (London, Sampson Low, Marston and Company, 1905).

Breytenbach, J.H. *Die Geskiedenis van die Tweede Vryheidsoorlog in Suid Afrika* Vol I (Pretoria, Die Staatsdrukker, 1969-1978).

Chisholm, R. *Ladysmith* (Johannesburg, Jonathan Ball, 1979).

Pakenham, Thomas. *The Boer War* (Johannesburg, Jonathan Ball, 1979).

Reitz, D. *Commando* (Johannesburg, Jonathan Ball, 1983).

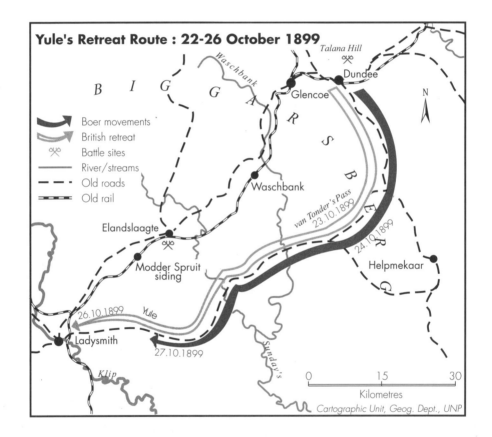